TO THE DAYS WHEN I AM BLUE

By Cloudwalker Weaver

Special Thanks to all who have helped me create this book;
to those whom I have written about;
and to you, for reading them.
I thank you most of all.

© 2018 Jacki Weaver. All Rights Reserved.

Author's Note

These are the poems that got me through confusion, weirdness, and doubt. Blue does not have to mean sad, and to me it doesn't—to me it means communication. So, these are to the days when I communicate.

They are broken into four sections: Love Poems, Poems for Thought and of Nature, The Weighted Things, and Randomness with a Pinch of Sincerity.

They are just that. Make of them what you will and what you want.

Anything can be taken to much greater depth if one feels the desire too; some of these poems were written for that and others were not, but all have meaning. Well, all but one. Though, it's meaning of not having meaning gives it meaning. Life is like that.

Love Poems About You

You

To the days when I am blue,
sad, down, and full of rue
when all I want is you,
but there is nothing I can do.
I hold my breath tight,
and try to put up a fight,
but despite all of my might,
some days... I lose.
some days I bruise,
some days I ooze,
some days I cruise.

but you are my light,
the reason for flight,
how I know everything will be alright.

Yes,
To the days when I am blue
sad, down and full of rue
it is then, I'll think of you
and how you looked in that view.

Weight of Water

I feel the water rising.
The artificial rain flowing over me and stopping into
my pool of thought.
 I watch the droplets hit the water,
  bounce s l o w l y back up.
Time seems to stop
I never want this rain to end.
    I want this tub to fill up over my head
      I want to swim up.
        I want to feel myself rising.
          I want to ascend.
 Floating here,
 feeling the water,
 how it falls.
I think of everything.
I form the most perfect of words,
 the most deft of sentences.
 I answer all of life's questions.
Here on the water,
 in the water,
with the water,
 I am the greatest of sages
 It is like I have sipped the warmest cup of tea,
  the one that makes you think the way you need to.

     I sink.
  Farther down into the depths of the rain.
I dive not wanting to be disturbed.
    I wait,
  waiting until I will know.
And I am afraid that I will never know.

Does everyone live with this feeling?
Have the millions before me sunk just as I do now?
I don't know how much longer I can wait?
 I don't know where I am going,
I don't know how I will get there.

 All I know is that I want you by my side.
    I want your honest words;
    I want your truth seeking eyes.
    I want your hands to find me and feel the truth for themselves.
 All I want is a life of stars and you.

I tower over my thoughts,
 and cower under my mind.
 Some days I don't know which is up.
But I know that tea is good,
and water hydrates the soul.
I know when to smile,
 and when to hug.
 I am not very good with appropriate,
but I can turn wonderful cart-wheels.

Of the stillness that seeps into my bones.
    Of the waiting that seems to be inherit with life.
Of the learning and re-learning.
    Of the never knowing.
 Of good-byes and surprise hellos.
    Of all of it, I would endure just for you.

Sonnet of Offering

Words lack and fail
  Tongue twisted and tied
yet, something so frail
  is to be warily eyed

When thoughts of you do enter,
  I admit suspense
Swirling like a storm centre
  yet much more intense.

Sometimes our paths do meet
  even though, we run the same race
However, it is something of bittersweet
  as we run a different pace.

The more I know you, the more I see,
so I will just smile and offer you tea.

Wit of Words

Wit of Words do want
yet,
Tongues do dance
with words of holy strife.
"What is life without gamble?"
whispers one tongue to an ear.
That ear lends the eye a leer.
The hands of the tongue
speak of nothing more than air from lung
and if those hands could
watch the eyes, they
would see a yielding truth.
something expressive
and a little uncouth.
That that ear would love
that tongue, if only
that tongue could hear.

An Attentive Gaze

Have you ever had a conversation with silence?
  The ebb and flow of the ideas
  swaying back and forth in such a way
  that you can say everything you have ever needed to say
  with only a glance?
And the lucky one who is looking at you,
  they know.
They know because they listen
  in such a way that is watching.
It is so much more different that any conversation you will ever have.
  In so many ways…it is better.
  In so many ways…it is worse.

Sinking into You

I'm sinking down into the blue
staring up and watching you
I've seen the way you move
I like the way you groove
the way you figure things out
leaves nothing left to doubt
your thoughts sing out across your face
I want to eat them and feel their taste
please let me know you more
I want to walk through your door

The Spots

There is a spot on my face
   something left out of place.
There is a hole in my heart
   left from when we part.
There is an emptiness
   filling me from within.
There is nothing
only a pulled pin.

Emotion left undone
   a battle lost; never won.
A hunger only felt from starvation
   yet, a plate avoided with frustration
these are the things that I feel.

It feels like I don't know how to be me,
like I am lost somewhere at sea

Footprints

    I think of that moment
where I followed your footprints
    How my foot fell
where yours had just been
    How your warmth had imprinted the earth
    How that warmth had sewn itself into my foot
as if it were a secret, meant only for me
as if my feet could follow your warmth any where you would wonder.
as if I were your shadow
    and you were my peter pan.

Holding in Air

    That moment when you realize that you are holding a breath.

    That relief that expands outward,
its fingers letting go of your chest.
The darkness fleeing from you,
escaping from the breath.
Scared of its life.
Exhaling that wispy last bit of dust.
It's so strange just how much that dust weighs.
A knowledge only dirty air brings.
While the fresh (sparkling) air brings balance to the lungs.
Every cell in the body feels grateful for the remembrance.
The air heats up in the lungs.
Creating a fire in which passion burns.
Creating a fire in which all things burn.

                Burning away fear
                Burning away dispair
                Burning away dis-ease
              Burning, Burning, Burning
          The fire eats the cool oxygen
      Leaving the lungs warm but hungry
          Reds, yellows, and oranges
            circulate within the chest
              I can see the warmth
                I can see the light
                  you are a beacon

The breath rushes out of the nostrils.
The air gushing like water.
up and out of the body

The lungs an empty pool.
Waiting for the next rush of air to feed the fire.
Waiting for the next gush of air to recede the shore.

A dammed amount of energy ,
   stored for special occasions.
Stored from when I'm next to you
    the flowing, the energy
      the dance, the movement
Just a small moment taken for memory
    for love
     for life
      for happiness

something to look at when I am alone
something to hold on to...like air

Words Failing to Fall

Damn sounds
   and how they resound.
Sticking in my throat
   and tripping on my tongue.
Letters swishing around in my mouth.
    Cleaning out what could have been.
Phrases falling from my lips,
   Falling like stones and staining the floor
 like blood from years before.

Waiting for the perfect moment,
   when you've already been given some.
Using other words that I don't need
   as a disguise
  just so you don't realize
but who am I fooling?
those around me?
or maybe?
    Just those between us.
Who knows what I am to say
or how I will get these words out
I am so scared that everyone will walk away.

Conformation

Two conversations
overlayed on top of one situation.
Constantly and consistently
waiting for conformation
of one thing or one mean
but neither is happening.
  which one is it?
 which could it be?
is it both?
   or am I crazy?

How could it be?
Is it ever so subtly?
Maybe I going off the deep end
  when everyone is talkin.
How will I ever know?

Maybe I should stand-up
  and make a show
  of who I am
  and what I know.

How I see you speaking in rhymes
and how you choose and decide.
Maybe I should just take everything at face value and

    stop reading between the lines
     stop checking out your eyes
      stop listening to the lies

Maybe I should accept that words can mean two things
and just hold on to the simplexidy of the situation.

Palaces within Palaces

Palaces within Palaces.
   Walls within Walls.
Places where golden beings float
   through mushroom halls.
Where drapes cover windows
   and intentions are misled.
Where thoughts beguiled
   and words are often left unsaid.

Palaces within Palaces.
   Colors over Colors.
Where lovers lie
   and cuddlers mingle
     with the prisms of blankets.
Where the heartstrings unbind
   and freely hang.
Yet, hoping and waiting to become a knot.
     Tangled up with your hue.
       Tangled up in bed with you.
         Tangled up through and through.
           Tangled in something I want to do.

Dancing in My Head

The world around me seems muted.
The lines soften into the objects.
The objects becoming distant,
but the colors.
Those stand out
making a pinwheel of emotions,
bright and crazed with the music.
A carnival of ideas cartwheel past
making room on the dance floor for more than one.
I glance a subtle look toward your direction;
the idea of you holds your hand gently waiting for mine.
We take the dance floor.
    With swishes and swashes
    With swooshes and sashays
    With swirls and swoops
Our feet go together like long lost friends.
They smoothly do as they please in unison.
This energy travels up through us,
into our hands where our bodies constantly met.
I can feel our movements working together
and I just continue to breathe.

    always breathe

You dip me low at just the right moment,
    giggles explode out of me
I can not control my glee,
    It flows out of me
Growing and pulsating into the other patrons.
    Bouncing about and absorbed by the others.

The mood elevates into a blissful bout of movement.
      everyone dances
Our bodies intertwine as we end the song.
I look into your eyes and see you glowing.
I feel the joy radiate from you.

Was this just a day dream?
Where are you?

Who are you to me?

Dualites
Separate moralities
Which one is the one?
Which mean do you mean?
What is this game you play?
Twice the meaning.
6 times the words.

dizzying, comprehending
spinning and living

Your words dance through my head.
Your scent confuses and frees.
Who are you to me?

Some maddening being
    birthed from the earth.
A wild thing
    that moves like leaves
A voice
    with the softness of a creek
and eyes that emit a fire.

I want to burn in your gaze
I need you to set me ablaze.

Eyes

Coming and Going,
Never quite knowing.
I cannot read what your eyes want me to hear,
Please speak it aloud and let it ring clear.
The air around us,
    bright with energy.
The air between us,
    electric and real

But your eyes.
    Your eyes are a pool.
Something for me to fall into.
A place I get caught by.
A space I cannot escape.
One where I am trapped by what they could mean
One where I am confused by how they seem.

Your eyes
I wish they would watch me
I want to feel them crawling over my skin.
make love to me, from a distance if you must.
but make love to me all the same.
I want to feel your eyes
enter me.
see me.
feel me.

Hands

Smoke drifts toward you,
like a magnet toward north.
You are the direction I wish to go.
You are my map and my goal,
My destination.

Your hands wrap around me.
Your legs part mine and keep me still.
Your fingers leave a trail that tingles;
    a sensation that I will feel far after the fact.

Your chest rumbles and I rub my face to it.
Your nose taps my forehead
and I become lost in you.
Its takes me days to find your face.

Your skin smells like its missed me,
I know I have missed it.
Your hands travel further,
making my topography shake.
You find my mound and gently stroke me
allowing me to overcome my fear.
Your touch is intoxicating.

The Whole of My Body

The whole of my body sings of your name
It waits, It wants
It plays your game.

You teases, You taunt.
the whole of my skin,
My mouth, Your lips.
nothing is sin.

The curve of my hips
rise and fall.
Nothing forgotten
you take it all.

   I hum forsooth,
      And the whole of my being whispers your truth.

Smell of You

You asked me today
if your sweater smelled ok
so I sniffed a snuff
and inhaled deeply the smell of you

you came fluttering into my nose,
as you have done since day one.
the scent of you sticks to me
and doesn't seem to want to fade
lasting with me through my day.

you smell good.
you smell like you
'tan and brown; like comfort and sunlight'
not like a pile of leaves
and not exactly like the trees
but wonderful and earthy
all the same.

you smiled that smirk
that sly half smile
it lights up your face
I can only assume
I have pleased you
when really,
    you pleased me.

A Blue-er Hue

Every little tiny hue, has a little hint of blue.
    Every little thing you do gives the world a blue-er hue
        Every little thing I see reverberates back to You to bring,
  The shiniest shade of Aquamarine pulsating

into
     and
         out of
             my view

    Spiralling up and giving truth.
      While a gold version of you cascades down,
     and gliding with your sounds

    The gold you plunges me over the edge of an azure cliff;
  Making everything blue in contrast of you.

Clouds of us

The clouds are blue
with a golden hue
splashing thru.
Allowing for the sun
to peek unto
leaving brightly light clues
for us follow.

Being a heightened model
and trying not to startle;
the sun's rays guide us into view
    It's a bit like me and a bit like you,
        that gold against that blue.

Clouds Finding Us

Clouds rolling away
White and Fluffy
Taking shapes
Leaving no sounds
Happily they float
    Waaaaay up high
Looking down on us.
Wishing we would come home,
giving us ideas and dreams.
Ever so softly
Guiding me
Guiding you
Guiding the two
    back together
        from the inbetween

If we were to follow them
as if they were some gem
whose reflection could show
just which way to go,
how long do you think it would be
until you finally met the me?

If seven maids with seven mops swept for half a year?
hmmm, what was your answer, my dear?

I am unsure I heard you
but I can surmise.

I know where we would be:
        in some place magnificent!

      some place gold and blue
    some place warm with hints of dew
a palace whose foundation lay firm
    a castle where we can learn
      a home made for two.
          a cave filled with fondue.

The clouds want us to come back,
to fly up and just walk.
Do you remember how they use to feel?
Under foot and under heel?
How the springy soft and full of light
felt against all your might?
My feet can still feel their wet
lingering and mingling with my sweat.

I know if I can just close my eyes long enough
I know if I just start walking
and hold your hand...

one day,
 We'll walk above the land
and the clouds will take us away.

Mesmerised

Mesmerised by your silent eyes.
Your movements speaking
   in rhythms and rhymes.
Spilling over onto the paper of my body.
Making me quiver with your caligraphy-ed eyelashes
   as they bat themselves up and down.
Creating long brush strokes and gentle lines.

My canvas over flows
   while your movements echo.
Our thoughts and our feelings
   both combined and intertwined.
Creating the art of dreams
And leaving everybody listening
   to our breath as we bow.

Eye level with the Clouds

In the clouds above clouds
that's where we'll lie.
To the clouds behind clouds,
that's where we'll hide.

Creating puffy, fluffy sculptures
of moistened air.
Living it up and watching the down there.
The swirling clouds bringing us closer.
The twirling mounds guiding me to the you
showing me what to do.

The great cotton balls casting cotton shadows.

as below; so above

like the cooing of my dove.
Brought to me by their every changing current.
The message they brings
rings of your love.
They whisper of your words
and deliver your well missed touch
as I am encompassed by them, they coo of you
your effervescent mist hand brings warmth to my
land.

Where are you?

Poems for Thought
and
Of Nature

Those Days

Sometimes the mind's eye is clear.
Others, it is clouded by wispy vapors of thought
coiling around the brain
    and spinning it out of control.
It behooves us to find that thought
    and to wait until it passes.
To watch it as it leaves.
To speed it on its way.
Leaving room and space for clarity to gain a footing.

Sometimes we must climb a mountain in order to be free.
Sometimes we must descend a flight of stairs
and stare into the void
in order to know ourselves better.

Those days are meant for oceans and plains
and other,
    far more,
        vast things.
Those days are meant for space.

Spirit Lake

The Spirit laps at my body.
  a washing away the grime
covering me completely
  and knowing of my crimes.
It cleanses and refreshes
  healing all my wounds.
It polishes me up
   like a silver spoon.

The Spirit swirls around my mind.
   creating deep and misty pools.
I wade right out and meet myself.
   the starting of a duel.
I tell myself of everything
  ending at the start.
we laugh about severity
   and it nearly breaks my heart.

We push out toward the silver sea
   with the spirit gently guiding me.
The ship, itself, made of scraps
  bits of us combined…
A thing of throw aways
  somehow frankensteined .
But she floats with understanding
  while laughter sets her sails.
She glides across the deepest part
  and sings out to the whales.

Heading straight for the shallow sea
  and just before we breach.
The whole of her begins to quake
 as if her bows were to break.
The shake spreads about her
  creating rough and choppy sea.
The thoughts of her wash over me,

'Can this really be?'

She is breaking down now;
   her boards have loosened up
while there is crying all around.

I throw myself about her
   and try to hold her tight.
Her terror and her fear
   are showing through the light.
She gives a final sigh
   and rips herself apart.

The Spirit laps at my body.

Kundalini

A serpent begins to uncoil.
Its body slowly moving upward and spinning.
    dancing this way and that way, with new energy.
     It glides ever further until it reaches your crown.
Here, it balances on its hind quarter bits.
    Balancing itself while dancing with the ultimate spirit.
    Balancing while dancing with gods and goddesses.
    Balancing while dancing with yourself.
There is no end to the golden rays.
    No end to the warm waters pouring over your shoulder.
    Soaking you.
Being absorbed into your being.
 It is forever flowing.
    You must first jump head first into the energy.
      You must trust it.
      Your own snake knows the way up.
It wants to dance with you.
   It always has.
   It always will.
      Let it.

Close your eyes
 and feel your snake sleeping at the base.
    Feel it coiled and fasting.
 It wants to eat.
    Feed it with your energy.
    Feed it with the energy of the world.
Let it help you to sustain yourself with oneness.
Remember that everything is an egg
Everything is both incredibly strong
      and incredibly fragile.

Remember the AND.

The all importance of equality
   and how despite being different;
     everyone and thing is truly just the same thing.
      Love.

Physical beings of love,
no matter how they all act;
   even if they do become corrupted...
Everyone holds the power to change.
     to grow.

Growing and becoming better that you were,
constantly evolving your mindset
constantly stepping into your un-comfort zone.

   The more un-comfortable you are with a situation,

     the more dangerous it can become.

The Space In-between

The space in-between dreams.
so fluid, so real
    Physical, yet impossible.
    Tangible, yet implausible.
    Inconsistent and ramshackled
    Incongruent and palpable

A world so sure of its own authenticity,
it could only be lying to itself.

It has been measured by:
    lines; graphs
    diagonals; parallels
    papers; inks
    meters; rhymes
    everything ending in s's.
So many plural forms
with so little time

Everything that is reality really isn't all that real.
True reality is masked by the senses.
A cloak made of what we feel.
A wound for us to heal,
and in order for us to see
and finally be free...
We must reach past our daily lives
and realize that it is all the dream
of some bigger thing.

Different Inks

Blank, like a page, I sat staring.
Waiting to be filled with overwhelming feelings.
Waiting to be filled with thoughts.
Waiting to be filled with things that do not matter to the me.
Waiting, just to see.

Blank, like a page, I try to remain.
Pushing out the feelings.
Pushing out the thoughts.
Pushing out with everything I've got.
Pushing and Pushing and Pushing.

A page with scribbles and drawings.
A page with lines and graphs.
A page with words and lovers.
A page, none the less.

You could fill whole books with your brain
but yet, all you do is complain.
Who is this you?
It is the me.
There is not a difference between the two
The You. The Me.
We are the same page,
but, We are different colored inks.

Water droplets fall

Water changes and falls.
Cascading down.
Becoming individuals;
but for only a moment
before splashing into their source.
Becoming one with their all.
Heading out toward the ocean
and living lives some places in-between.

Flowing over rocks
and picking up leaves.
The debris taking the particles hostage
distracting them from their course.
Pooling out trains of thought,
stagnating in speculation,
eddying in anticipation
and whirlpool down in reflection.
Eroding away at that which can not be changed.
Leaving little patterns of conclusions ,
pathways of delusions
and breadcrumbs for us to follow.

If ever we were to swallow;
The truths of Us
The lies of Us
and see clearly into the depth of Us.

The safety of the edge only allows us the shiny
but never teaches us to swim.
Never teaches us to dive.
The one who stays on the beach
can not hold their breath for very long,
often losing their patience and peace
after wading out only waist deep.

The frozen water allows us only onto the surface
skating around, but never fully knowing
what it is we have been holding on to.

A depth so great that whales could live in lakes.
    A deepness so vast one is left flabbergast
        An expanse so profound that understanding is as
easy as breathing,
        and acceptance is first nature.

Water droplets fall,
Filling us up with our own source.

Encased

Glittering, Glimmering, Gleaming
   Shiny, Shimmery, Seeming
All perfectly reflecting and clinging.
The leaves are encased with fros.t
They glisten under the street lamps.
Do you think it keeps them warm?
That frozen blanket shutting out all world
protecting from the rest of the elements.
Keeping the green green.
Freezing it in time.
Magnifying what's inside.
Letting it be while the rest of the world wilts with the cold
and changes into a wasteland of ice.

The ice blossoms into a frozen flower.
Blooming to perfection in the twilight.
The cluster twinkles.
The smallest rainbows find their way into my eye.
They dance around.
Making shadows of warmth.

Nothing lasts.
Nothing is encased forever.
Even the ice will melt.
Even the snow will become grass.
The cold will fight back to stay,
but the warmth will win the day
The inner fire will dissolve the crystallized winter
and boil it to steam.

The Sun

The sun looks down from the sky.
Its rays gently play with the dust in the air.
Leaving a shinning path and a dazzling dance in its wake.
Particles rising.
Swishing this way.
Turning that.
Being dipped into and out of the golden light.
The hems on their extaordinairly tiny dresses sashay to and fro.
Leaving dust bunnies with dreams of heaven.

Water Slides Across the Land

The water slides across the land.
Making its way, as only it can.
Using itself to make its own path.
Carving out a road for future self to know,
just exactly where to go.
Never having fear of run-over or flood.
Never questioning the day of dwindling;
knowing that it will always recede yet still be the road.

The only way the path will fade is if we fill it with greed.

The water knows its direction
and will always heads that way.
It will stop and pool for a bit
resting and relaxing,
eddying out to hold branches and trees in its soft embrace.
Then it will flow and flow and flow and over fill
    until
the water falls
  cascading down
    dancing in the air
      jumping with such a flare
        frolicking with no compare
          finding total individualism in being one tiny drop
            before coming back together
              into the oneness of the stream
It is always the same water,

    yet,
It will always be different drops of life.
Finding its own story.
Finding its own strife.
Allowing space between each drop.
Confessing its love for each bit of itself.
Calmly waiting for itself to return back to itself.
Knowing that the tales it will bring,
will always ring in your ears.
Leaving you deafened by its beauty.
Leaving you in awe of how the whole flow works.
Leaving you in understand...
    that everything is an 'AND'

Thoughts on a Flight

I find myself walking on clouds.
    It feels Natural.
        It feels wonderful.
            It feels as if I am stationary
                while the world slides by unheeded.

Almost lazy. Almost without care.
I watch as it turns and I remain.

A fly landing on a soap bubble.

The shadow cast down from above.
    As below so above.
Falling into that shadow but only from above
as below is where that shadow lie.

Staring clouds in the face.
 Reaching out and connecting.
Staring clouds in the eyes.
 Reaching out and feeling.

The green oceans of land.
 Large tracts of sea waiting to be freed.
 Rolling into thundering waves of mountains
 and washing up on the shores of homes.

Majestic Summit of Clouds

Majestic Summit of Clouds
cascading far beneath me
solid enough to touch, yet
just out of reach.

My fingers brush the edge of my window
and lift me out of my seat.
I'd fall through your
crisp vapors before I'd fly.

Yet,
  I would still
  venture forth for flight.

  Falling is a kind of flying, after all.

Clouds Today

Have you seen the clouds today?
How they wonder this-a-way?
Crawling over walls
and sliding slightly over malls.
Leaving thoughts dismantled
and words channeled .
Going and flowing with your brain.
Leaving nothing but remains.
They cast a shadow from above.
They cast it down but with love.
They want to shade you in such a way.
They want to take you without dismay
for you to grow, you must be watered.

Rain falls from them,
giving you the emotion you require
to receive everything you desire.
Sinking into your roots.
Drowning out the fear,
allowing the dirt to draw near.
Nurturing you.
Nourishing you.
Loving the whole of you.

Have you seen the clouds today?
They have watched the way you sway,
   dancing with the trees
      and talking with the bees
but now let the clouds grab your thoughts.
Give them the center of your dot.
Understand what they've brought, then allow them to
float off too

and be nothing more than just the you.

Waterfall Day

Fresh green moss,
growing beside the falls.
Vibrant verdant floss,
existing next to you.
Reaching out with its fuzzy tendrils.
Wanting for your caress.
Loving the moment you notice it
and place it upon your dress.

The moss is greener here, greener than I ever knew.
Glowing and Bright.
Guiding you (away from night)
to the place you need be.
Giving your feet a place to rest.
Just before the journey picks back up again.
Oh how, the moss is your friend.
So soft
So loving
So much apart of you
Allow it to help
Aake root in your soul
Allow yourself to glow

The trails we follow are those of other beings.
Cut through and made into a path.
hard, packed earth.
Lots of feet have been here.
Lots of being lost.
Lots of being found.
Lots and Lots of Lots,
Growing up from the ground.
If you are silent enough

and stand very still,
you can see the feet
packing down the earth.
You can feel the awe
that grow with the leaves.
You can hear the music of the trees.
Of it all listen.
Never forget to listen.
You can hear everything in a symphony of life.

Distemper'd Tempest

The Clouds are Heavy
The Air
Thick and Malleable
Impending Rain
hangs stagnant
waiting to
    w a s h   a w a y

The Clouds turn black
and rather angry.
Lightening frightens the sky
    So Bright
        So Hand Like
  grasping and in fists
 touching tall trees
feeling with electricity

The Clouds scream
at the earth
  making it quake with its clay.
Their volume invades
leaving rattled bones
in their wake.

Cold breath stirs leaves.
blowing them:
   Back and Forth
     back and forth

Concentric little circles
with confused leaves falling.
Hail takes up courage
and pelts the Soil.
Its anger imprints
and soon builds.

The world weeps
upon itself
rending itself
in twain
leaving Nothing
not even Rain.

Day Falls into Night

And day slowly falls into night.
Splashing about yellows and greys.
The night comes on quick,
as if to say something less enduring about the day.
The night feels good on my skin.
The way it rests and sinks in.
See the wind and how it flows?
Its currents brushing back
the restraint of the day.
Feel the dark with its looming question mark.
Its black velvet brings out languish
yet, revels a simple wish.

Here, we play.
We find our way.
We venture forth
   and claim the world.

And then...night slowly fades, gradually, back to day.
The blues and blacks fight for that joyous night
but alas the pinks and reds win out overhead.

The day people being to stir while we retreat to bed.
With our lasting aware sigh, we sing unto the day
'oh enduring sprite, what a wonderful night.'

Dervish

Shift, Slide, Spin
The world turns into stripes of colors.
The colors make an egg.
The egg just turns and turns.
Waiting for the eyes to stop so the world can make sense.
Waiting and Waiting
but waiting in vain.

The world doesn't make sense.
Even when I stop spinning,
Even when the dizzy subsides,
the world doesn't make sense.

I can see it turning
I can see you turning
and I recongize my own desire to turn.
Thoughts are blurred into the background.
Everything is one.

The fabric was made for this.
The edges welling up freely and floating down fiercely.
Turning (spinning) in circles.
Turning (spinning) with grace.
Turning (spinning) with delight.

and then,
as if the weight of the world had been laid out on my skirt
the colors collapse into sharp shapes.
Images appear,

sliding into the 3rd dimension.
Lines become visible, hard edges too.
Everything is separate.
Nothing makes sense.

Nothing has always made sense.

Human Society from a Different Angle

A species that has grown to find discomfort with unity and strives to be separated from each other.
    Compare and Contrast
    Scrutinze and Examine
    Rate and Vote
'You are only who you look like' is the underlying message.
The only effort is really just make-up; it's a game changer.

We are a breed of beings looking only at the decoration and never behind the eyes.
It's upseting, really, but intelligence lacks.
We degrade what our species truly stands for with hate and
it eats our souls with a slow but frightening hunger.
We have not brought this on ourselves;
it is not our fault that we deem ourselves lower, apologizing for being born, on a regular basis.
we are taught one thing and then never shown the strength to actually do it.
our parents could never be to blame.
 how dare us to ever think they could be weak,
never regarding the fact that one has to be weak in order to be strong.
Never regarding perception and
only seeing the problems one way.
Never realizing that one-dimensional thought is a weakness.

Uncomfortable with the idea that it's all just one thing.
It's all just alive.
Instead we have to focus on our differences,
Without celebration of them.

What. A. Strife.

Damnation Blues

Damnation blues
sent from the all-mighty high.
Where the floating folks look down with hopes,
knowing you could never
live up to their wants and desires.
Knowing you could never be them
but hoping that you'd find a way.
That you'd gradually become a drop in their ocean.

Salvation Hues
All bright and brimming with dues.
It is in that day,
maybe somewhere hidden away,
where you will find yourself standing.
Letting wave upon wave affect you,
and at some point the hidden will reveal.
That you will always be splashed by waves.
That you will never recede to attack to recede to attack.
That you do not want to beat things into a new shape.
That you are not the waves.

Nor are you a single drop
   in some one else's ocean
Nay, you are your own body of water
   with your own boundless depth.

The Weighted Things

Tugged Skirt

I can feel you holding on to my skirt.
your fingers grasping at the fabric;
wanting to hold on forever.
The folds knotting
and creating weight.

You clutch at my hem,
bringing imbalance
and leaving me lopsided.
My path is no longer mine.
My feet cannot see the way.
You must let go for me to finally stay.

But your hands are now tangled
and every chance for me to pull away,
rips my skirt
and leaves me bare.

I can no longer care
or be scared
of the cold the rips bring.
I must face it
and
I must face it alone.

My feet must be free,
only then will the cold warm me.

Miscommunication is Ripe

Are we sinking?
Are we floating?
The two of us,
Living in the ultimate paradox.
Flying but fighting.
Fighting but flying.
The tears drip hot
Molten salt runs away from my eyes.
Moistens my lips and hair.
You say one thing and yet mean another.
I say one thing and still you hear another.
Where am I?
My paradise has a transposed hell upon it.
I am drowning in my feathers.
I have seemingly cut off your wings,
chained and bound you to me,
Now you need permission to fly?
Now you need to ask me why?

I have no answer,
for all of my words,
for all of my thoughts,
have they been nothing but encouraging?
Am I killing you with my love?
Are you destorying yourself?
Is there a fault?

Miscommunication is ripe,
take the apple and bite.
Let its confused juices in.
Dripping down from your chin
and into my own mouth.
The clarity is lacking.
Nothing left but our own smacking.

A haze has settled
and nothing I say
nothing I do
is right.
It must be corrected.
It must be spoken about.
Like a dog who disobeyed its master.
Like a whore who has run away from the whorehouse
and has no idea about the world.

Waves of you and the weight of me.

The feelings come in waves, as they should.
Surmounting and drowning out all of the senses.
Leaving me overwhelmed by my own choices.

I have this sense that everything will not be ok
I have this feeling that everything will now change.
That the openness will either strengthen us or destroy us.
I can not be in closed-ness.
  I must be open.
    I must have the air
      I must know the water
        I must dance with the flame
          I must be buried underneath the weight of my own stones.
my stones, your stones, our stones.
    These Stones.
The things the weigh me down.
The rocks in my pocket as I walk out into the river
of the knowing and the coming and the going.
Alas I sink into the water,
At last, I wade out into the sea.

At first I thought it was just something for me to drown in.
Something for me to be lost on.
but I have been so lost for so long within my own self that I now welcome the feeling.
I have been wanting and waiting for this moment for a while.

I have chased after shadows and dreams
I have become those things
I have seen you and watched from afar
I have been pre-occupied by your body
I have lost so much space
I have lost so much.
I have lost.

Yet, I have gained.
Does the gain outweigh the loss?
Or is it the other way?
It's a lot of weights.
It's never an 'or' situation, only and always an 'AND'.
you are me 'AND' I am you
you are he 'AND' he is me.
we are all the same 'AND' we are different.

Floating in a different Direction

Panels of water; Crazy shades.
Pelting down gently yet in a haphazard way.
Causing mass flooding but bringing hydration to droughts.
Ponding and pooling to make a place,
where our boats float rock back and forth.
waiting for us to make-up our minds.
Foolish boats.... they will be waiting for sometime while we paddle around.

    Piddle paddle.
      Piddle paddle.
        Piddle paddle.
I wouldn't have this any other direction.
I am lost but as long as I am lost with you; it's not so bad.
But there you go.
Paddling on your way.
Going toward some greater destination.
Some greater pie in the sky.
Maybe that is what you need
    someone who isn't too much
    someone who does not overload you
    someone who learns the way you learn and
moves at your pace.
I am tired of running.
I am tired of slowing.
I am tired of this game we are continually playing.
I just want you to be so secure in you that I don't play that large of a role.

the responsibility is killing me
...or at least it feels like a knife in my chest
something to cut off my wings.
Please let me fly.
I want the freedom with the limitations.
why can I not have both?
Everything is an 'AND' nothing is an 'OR'.
Everything. Nothing.

Humans are a large contradiction;
always second guessing themselves.
That is the highest proof of the sacred 'AND'.

How long should we wait?

The day turned to night
    It was waiting for you to break but since you never did, it went ahead anyways.
It thought it was absurd to hold the whole world up just for one person,
No matter how important that person was....
  There was after all the great likely hood of you never breaking.
  of you just simply waiting.
waiting, waiting, waiting

  It knew this and decided it better to not wait.
so it sank
  and having fallen toward the horizon,
  it left the world a warm, encompassing black.
One that, both, pressed upon and freed you.
And still, offered you direction.
So it sent you smells;

  The smells that drifted toward you and upward into you,
  rang out of days past.
  Birthday candles, the prickle of static,
and softly floating there, gently through the air, was a whiff of someone long gone, yet one you havent met.
    A comforting sniff, filling you with awe and wonder.
      You can't place this person
         but you know you've smelled this smell
           a million and more times.

Where are you?
Who are you?
I will no longer wait,
What direction must I walk?

Thick Like Molasses

I feel your weight agaisnt me.
Your strength pulls my weight agaisnt you.
Our heaviness pours over everything,
    thick molasses dropping from a height
and dripping onto the world.
Covering and darkening the light
 What am I to do?
It is these moments which I dream of.
These moments where I want to live, to stay, to be.
These moments, where we stick together and stick to everything.
Leaving a lasting imprint of nutrients.

But these moments are fleeting.
They skeeter away,
like marbles on uneven floor.

The greatness followed by the hollow.
The weight followed by the weightless.
 Are we sinking or floating?

Cracked From Sounds

Loud and long sound waves hit each other.
Reverberating back and hitting their owners.
I am hurting myself, screaming into the night.
You are hurting yourself, becoming louder than you ever have.
We scream so that the other would hear.
Our words shooting fast, like a fighter pilot
over a huge and vast chasm that has opened up
and gobbled at us until we can no longer see each other.
Despite being right beside each other.
I only want to whisper to you,
I only want to hear your soft words.
Instead, neither one of us understands the other
and instead of trying to word it differently
or speaking in a gentler manner
or thinking anything about how we used our words;

we yell it,
over and over and over and over again.
Until our throats run sore
and we cough blood.
Until our ears are cracked from our sounds
and deafened by our own delusions.
Until the world is washed in our tears and we have nothing left,
Not even each other.

Randomness
With a pinch of Sincerity

Word Doodles

Noodles
Doodels
Ka-boodles
Hyphenated struddles
What is life?
Why do we sail it?
Sinking, Sinking, Sinking

Downward to the tub
blub, rub, stub
maybe?
perchance?
How come?

Dadelus
modelus
Foadelus
What are you?
Where did you
Fly from?
Sinking ships
with lack-a-dasies
No sealing wax
No shoes
How about cabages?
How about kings?
How could we be
if there is none
to be?

Love Between a Spider and Her Fly

In my mind, it is you I see.
Weaving a web of wonders
A beautiful spider who has entrap'd me.
Something truly worth the ponders

You slowly turn me over,
Sticky and almost fed
Am I now your trused lover?
or just something for your bed.

Am I to be bleed dry?
or allowed my precious insides?
Alas, no matter the voice of why
You always take me in your strides.

But a love between a spider
and her fly must always expire.

Hidden

the paradox of life
tries to hide
in sea shells and pies
but loves to ride
with sunglasses and highs
leaving out nothing,
not even the truth of the lie
the happiness of a cry
the answering of why

Dear Red,

"Red and blue,
Me and you"
Her sounds cascading down and rooting me to the ground.
Sense mingles with nonsense producing the most delicate of words.
Fragile and Lovely,
like a frozen flower held perfectly still refracting the red and the blue.
The me and The you.
With dots glued and eyes shaped, everything with its place.
 We created a perfect space,
where our colors combined
and a vibrant purple escaped.

If it's us against the world; then we shall bring the color to it.
No more boring or drab.
Only giggles and opulence.

You are not an empty jewelry box, my red.
YOU are the tiny delicate drawers with well crafted sliding doors,
filled to the brim with crimson jewels.
You are not just the whole box,
but also the smallest most complex parts.
YOU are the design of the thing, the love the creator brings.
You are the paint covering yourself, the woven lattice, the hinges.
You are the glue holding yourself together better than anyone else
In a glorious fashion.

And you do not stop there.
You are the things you place inside your beautifully chambered walls
and that's the most important part.
Because you are the box that chooses;
which jewels go where, if they go at all.
It's your delicate fingers, and yours alone,
that decide what to wear or
if something is not for play today.

My dearest Red with the gleaming dot
 whose eyes mesmerize
and whose smile is an invitation to mischief,
I love you.
Sincerely,
Blue.

Leafing

Look at the shapes on the window.
    Look at them crawling.
The dimension of them seems to jump off the wall into our world.
Creating shadows of its own and moving in time with the leaves.
    Bustling this a way and that a way.

A few of the yellow, waxy leaves fall to the grounding.
Wanting to be caught, yet loving the chase.
    A stag in motion.
    A boundless ocean.
The wind unknowingly sending wishes scattering everywhere.
Brushing up against the pavement and dealing with being trampled underfoot.
    If only a hand had caught the leaf!
        If only, If only, If only.
Alas, no hand was there and the leaves continued to float ever so slowly,
like the trees had planned it that way.

Silly trees, planning out their leafing.

I guess it is a good idea... to read the situation and then leaf it accordingly.
    Just to float ever so gently away from the top all the way down until you are hidden.

Sleepy Little Houses

Sleepy little houses,
All sleeping in tiny row
with their windows at half a glow.

Sleepy little houses,
cozier than they seem.
Waiting around to dream.
A big thing.
A warm place for you to lean.

Sleepy little houses,
offering you security,
giving you comfort,
and wishing you would only dream
and do nothing

Cozy and waiting
for sleep to come
the doors are all shut
against the bitting cold of thought.

DREAM THE THINGS

Dream of mad Monkeys,
Dream of their King,
Dream of peach banquets,
Dream of gold rings,
Dream of beauty, its hair raven red.
Dream of stars and travel, love and bed
Let not a terror stir in your head.
Let no evil rise up the dead.
Allow no horror to torment, my dear.
Be calm your vision will clear.
Now dream of all things,
but dream them good.

Underwater Sheen

Underwater sheen
tiny bubbles
clinging to your stubble
like delicate armor
 glistening; glimmering
tiny pockets of air
held on to your hair
like wispy, vaporous diamonds
 glittering; glowing

floating upwards
  shifting upwards
    fizzing upwards

Rising to the surface
wavering to the sky
zigzagging along
and tickling your spine

FIVE

5 White Cows
waiting by my path.
Staring into me,
with 10 pools of mystery.
Following me,
asking me this,
stating that,
p a i e n t l y waiting
for my reply.

5 Alabaster Bovine
leading me astray
or showing me the way?
preceving knowlegde
I'll never know.
Boring the importance
into my soul.
Eyes widen from recognition.

5 colorless moo's
in fact, listening, to you.
Curiosity and love abounds.
They, do in fact, understand your sounds.

A-Maze

I am walking through a haze,
my head is a maze.
What will I find
within my mind?
A happy little place?
Or some sad empty space?
A vast blue ocean?
Or just the same motion?
A palace of gold?
Or growing black mold?
Oh, what will I find
deep within my mind.

and when I find my way,
only I can say,
who I will be,
when I am free.

Lines in the Sand

Green lines drawn in the sand
Blue lines drawn in water
Yellow lines drawn in the air
Red lines drawn in the embers

The places you get to are the ones you were going.
Try not to second guess where you are.
Know that you are there due to these lines.
They pull you.
They push you.
They drag you out into the road
and watch as you are run over and over and over.

These lines wrap you up
and take you were you need to go.
Never fear the lines.
Never fear the paths.
Never fear the cars.
Always show courage and overcome.
You are amazing.
You will do just fine.
You can make everything out of nothing.
You are the wow.
You are the wonder.
and if not....then just laugh because you know the truth of the matter is that.....
You are the woah.

To the Nights when I am blue

Today doesn't feel real.
Today is given a dream like quality,
a certain feel in the air,
Reminds of what remains to be.
I stand here thinking,
the past, the future;
and never quite linking.

My mind jumbled
not a straight line.

and then there was you,
as there has always been
ringing quite true
and brimming with skin.

A shinning knight
but with added flavor.
An angel in flight
who frequently waivers .
A man with a fight.
A man of the night.
The one whose steadiness
comes from my plight.

painted, a mess and still wishing for you.

To the nights when I am blue,
   with my vision all askew
      here I stand,
         somewhat Cerulean.

Fin.